Text and illustrations copyright © 2018, 2020 by Chris Ferrie

Cover and internal design © 2020 by Sourcebooks

Cover and internal design by Will Riley

Sourcebooks and the colophon are registered trademarks of Sourcebooks.

All rights reserved.

Published by Sourcebooks eXplore, an imprint of Sourcebooks Kids

P.O. Box 4410, Naperville, Illinois 60567–4410

(630) 961-3900

sourcebookskids.com

First published as Red Kangaroo's Thousands Physics Whys: *The Light of the Rainbow: Optics*
in 2018 in China by China Children's Press and Publication Group.

Library of Congress Cataloging-in-Publication Data is on file with the publisher.

Source of Production: PrintPlus Limited, Shenzhen, Guangdong Province, China

Date of Production: February 2020

Run Number: 5017785

Printed and bound in China.

PP 10 9 8 7 6 5 4 3 2 1

Let's Make a Rainbow!

Seeing the Science of Light with Optical Physics

sourcebooks
eXplore

#1 Bestselling
Science Author for Kids
Chris Ferrie

While playing outside, Red Kangaroo notices a rainbow in the sky.

"How beautiful!" she says. "I wonder if Dr. Chris will know what makes all those colors."

"Dr. Chris," says Red Kangaroo when she gets to the lab, "Can you tell what makes a rainbow?"

"That's easy," Dr. Chris replies. "All it takes is water and light!"

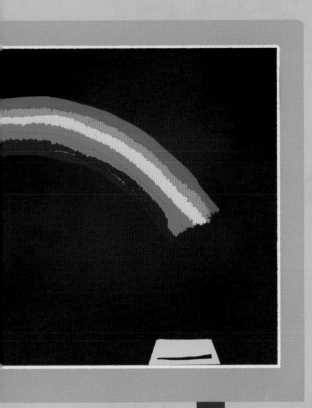

"No way!" says Red Kangaroo. "Please show me!"

"Sure!" says Dr. Chris. "But first you need to know about **optical physics**."

"First I need to teach you about how light moves," says Dr. Chris. "**Light** always travels in a straight line."

"A straight line?" cries Red Kangaroo. "That's so boring! I like to bounce all around!"

"Don't worry, light isn't boring!" Dr. Chris says. "It travels in a straight line until it hits something. Then three different things can happen to the light."

"I bet I can guess the three things!" says Red Kangaroo.

"Imagine if some light comes in and hits a block. What do you think happens to the light?" Dr. Chris asks.

"I know! The block will stop the light!" Red Kangaroo responds.

"That's right!" says Dr. Chris. "When light gets stopped by something, that is called **absorption**."

"Now imagine light hits a smooth or shiny surface like a mirror. What do you think happens to the light then?" Dr. Chris asks.

"The light bounces back!" says Red Kangaroo.

"Exactly! This is called **reflection**," Dr. Chris says. "But mirrors aren't the only things that help reflect light. Every object we can see reflects light. Otherwise we wouldn't be able to see them!"

"Wait a minute," says Red Kangaroo. "But light from the Sun or a lightbulb looks white to me. If everything reflects light, then why is this apple red instead of white? Why isn't everything white?"

"What a great question!" Dr. Chris replies. "Light holds all the **colors** in it. Different objects reflect different colors for our eyes to see. All other colors get absorbed by the object so our eyes can't see them. That apple is red because it reflects red light, and a yellow apple looks yellow because it reflects yellow light!"

"Let's move on to the last thing light can do," Dr. Chris says.

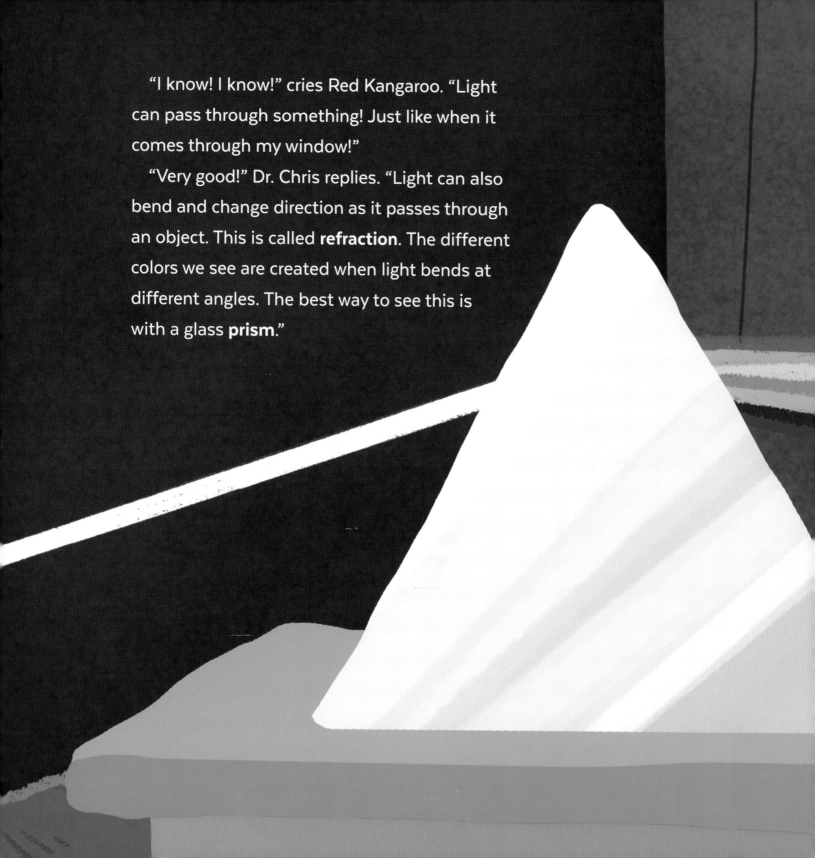

"I know! I know!" cries Red Kangaroo. "Light can pass through something! Just like when it comes through my window!"

"Very good!" Dr. Chris replies. "Light can also bend and change direction as it passes through an object. This is called **refraction**. The different colors we see are created when light bends at different angles. The best way to see this is with a glass **prism**."

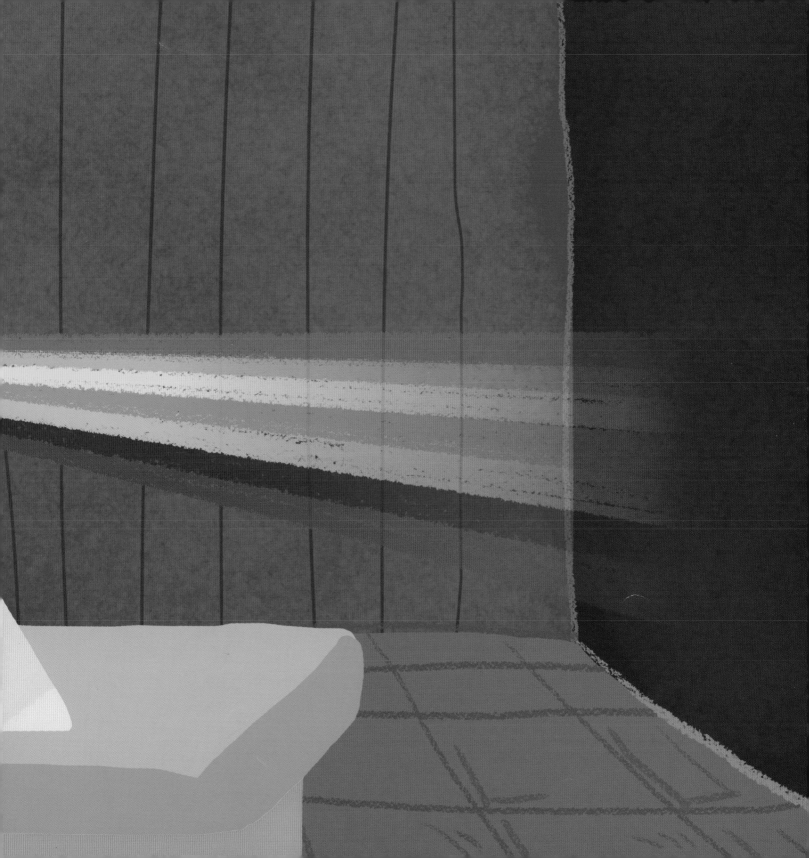

"I don't have a prism at home," says Red Kangaroo. "But I've seen light bend when I use a straw in a glass cup!"

"Great example, Red Kangaroo!" says Dr. Chris. "The easiest place to observe light refracting is when light goes into water."

"You've mastered the three ways light moves. Now we can talk about how to make a rainbow!" Dr. Chris says. "When it rains, sunlight passes through the raindrops. All the different colors break apart inside the raindrops."

"That's because the light is refracting!" says Red Kangaroo.

"Exactly!" says Dr. Chris. "Then some of that light is reflected."

"Also inside the raindrop?" asks Red Kangaroo.

"That's right," replies Dr. Chris.

"And then the light refracts a second time before coming out of the raindrop as..."

"A beautiful **rainbow**!" cries Red Kangaroo.

"But what if it's not raining?" Red Kangaroo asks. "Is there a way I can still make a rainbow?"

"Sure you can!" Dr. Chris says. "With a water hose, we can watch the sunlight reflect and refract!"

"Yay! Now I know how to make my own rainbow!" says Red Kangaroo. "Thanks for teaching me optical physics, Dr. Chris!"

Glossary

Absorption
When light hits an object and stops moving. The object takes in (absorbs) the energy of light.

Color
Different energies of light that our eyes can see. Colors are created when light refracts and breaks apart at different angles.

Light
Energy that travels very quickly in a straight line. Most of the light we see comes from the Sun.

Optical physics
The science of light and how it interacts with things.

Prism
An object with a triangular shape that is generally made of glass or other clear materials.

Rainbow
The breaking up of white light into different colors when the light refracts and reflects in drops of water.

Reflection
When light bounces back after it hits a surface. Shiny surfaces are good at reflecting light.

Refraction
When light bends as it passes through an object.

Show What You Know

1. Name the three things that light can do when it hits something.

2. Describe the difference between refracting and reflecting.

3. Count how many reflections and refractions happen inside a raindrop to create a rainbow.

4. Explain why a red apple looks red even though sunlight is white.

5. You may have noticed that a rainbow is made up of seven colors. These colors always appear in the exact same order. Can you list them from top to bottom?

Answers on the last page.

Test It Out

What color is an apple?

1. You will need an apple, a flashlight, rubber bands, and different colors of tissue paper. One piece of tissue paper should be the same color as your apple.

2. Fold each piece of tissue paper three or four times so that it will cover the face of the flashlight. Each tissue paper color will help you create different colored light.

3. Make a prediction about what color the apple would reflect if you were to shine different colored light on it. You should have a prediction for each color of tissue paper that you hold over the flashlight beam.

4. Take one of your folded papers and secure it over the face of the flashlight using a rubber band.

5. Clear some space off a table for you to place the apple. Then turn off the lights.

6. Turn on the flashlight and shine it on the apple.

7. Record your observation. Is the apple the same color as before or is it now reflecting a different color?

8. Repeat for the other colors of tissue paper. Continue to record your observations. Were your predictions correct?

Try this experiment with other objects. You can also try experimenting with shining two colors onto the objects if you have more than one flashlight!

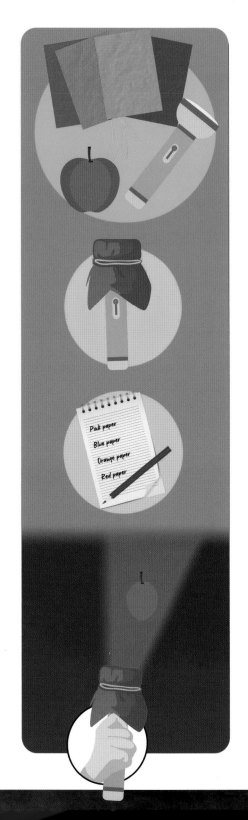

Which way refraction

1. You will need a large glass cup and a piece of paper.

2. Draw two arrows in the middle of the paper. Both arrows should point left and should be about as long as the width of the glass cup. Leave about an inch or two between the two arrows.

3. Hold your picture behind the cup so that you can look at the arrows through the glass. Do the arrows look the same as before? Predict what would happen to the picture if the cup were filled with water.

4. Fill the glass cup with water.

5. Hold the picture behind the glass again. You will want to position it so that you can see only the lower arrow through the water. Record your observation. Does it look as you predicted?

6. Try holding the picture so you can look at both arrows through the water. What happens now?

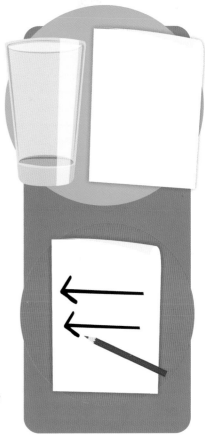

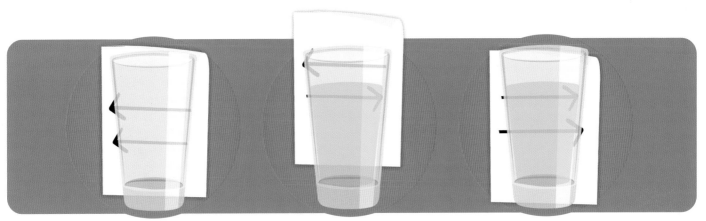

Try looking at your picture through other clear objects that light can pass through, like a window or plastic. Does the picture change or look different?

What to expect when you Test It Out

What color is an apple?

With the lights off, your eyes will probably not be able to see any color. The apple will probably just look like a shadow. White light contains all the colors, so you can't make a flashlight shine only one color at a time (even with different colored tissue paper). A red apple can only reflect red light and changing the color of the light won't change that fact. Certain colors of tissue paper will let enough white light pass through so that the apple can be seen. But the apple will still reflect the same color it was before you turned off the lights.

Which way refraction

The picture should look mostly the same when you look at it through the empty glass. But the arrows will flip directions and point right when you look at them through water. Light bends when it passes through most clear things but it bends even more when it passes through thick, round objects (like the water in the glass cup, or even the eyeglasses that Dr. Chris wears).

Show What You Know answers

1. Absorption, reflection, and refraction.

2. When light reflects, it bounces off an object. When light refracts, it passes through the object and bends.

3. Two refractions, one reflection.

4. The red light is reflected and all the other colors are absorbed.

5, Red, orange, yellow, green, blue, indigo (a color that's a mix of blue and purple), and violet (another name for purple).